Aa

Avocado

B b

Broccoli

This book is designed for children between the ages of 2 and 4, but it's also a great resource for parents, teachers, and caregivers looking for fun and engaging ways to teach the alphabet.

So come along with us on this alphabet adventure, and let's discover the wonder and magic of letters together!

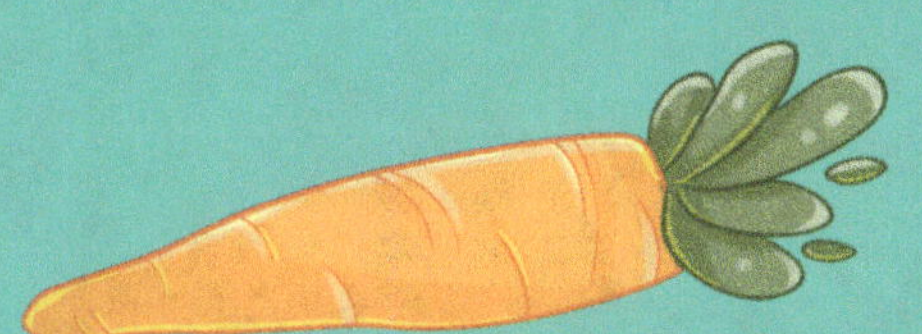

Tianah forest

The aim of this book is to **introduce capital and small letters to young children while teaching them the names of fruits and vegetables.**

C c

Carrots

D d

Dates

E e

Eggplant

F f

Fennel

G g

Ginger

H h

Honeydew melon

I i

iceberg Lettuce

J j

Jackfruit

K k

Kale

Leeks

M m

Mango

Nn

Nectarine

Orange

P p

Pepper

Q q

quince fruit

R r

rhubarb

S s

sweet potatoes

T t

Tomatoes

Uu

ugni berry

Valencia Orange

Ww

Watermelon

X x

Extra portion of vegetables

Xigua a type of watermelon

Y y

Yams

Z z

zucchini